Emotions can feel strange.

So these colourful creatures are here to help.

They have emotions from happy to sad.

They will show you that all emotions are okay!

I'm happy.

And that's okay.

When you are happy you might want to...

Talk

Sing

Smile

You might feel awake.

You might want to see your friends.

You might want to hug people.

You might feel happy if it's a special day like your birthday.

When you are sad you might want to...

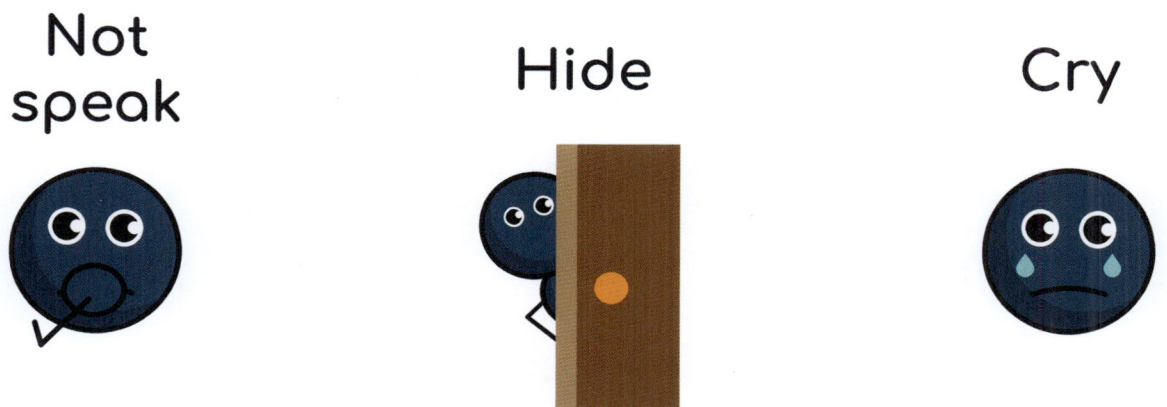

You might **feel sleepy**.

You might **have a hurt head**.

You might **feel unhappy**.

You might feel sad if your friend has moved to a new town.

When you are shy you might want to...

Not speak

Hide

Look at the floor

You might feel like not talking.

You might feel scared.

You might feel like hiding.

You might feel shy if you meet someone new.

When you are excited you might want to...

Talk

Jump up and down

Sing

You might feel awake.

You might feel like running around.

You might feel happy.

You might feel excited if you are going on holiday.

When you are confused you might want to...

Not speak

Hide

Look at the floor

You might feel scared.

You might feel silly.

You might feel sad.

You might feel confused if you need to answer a hard maths question.

I'm grumpy.

And that's okay.

When you are grumpy you might want to...

Moan

Hide

Do nothing

You might feel lazy.

You might feel like not talking.

You might feel angry.

You might feel grumpy if you have to do something you don't want to.

I'm surprised!

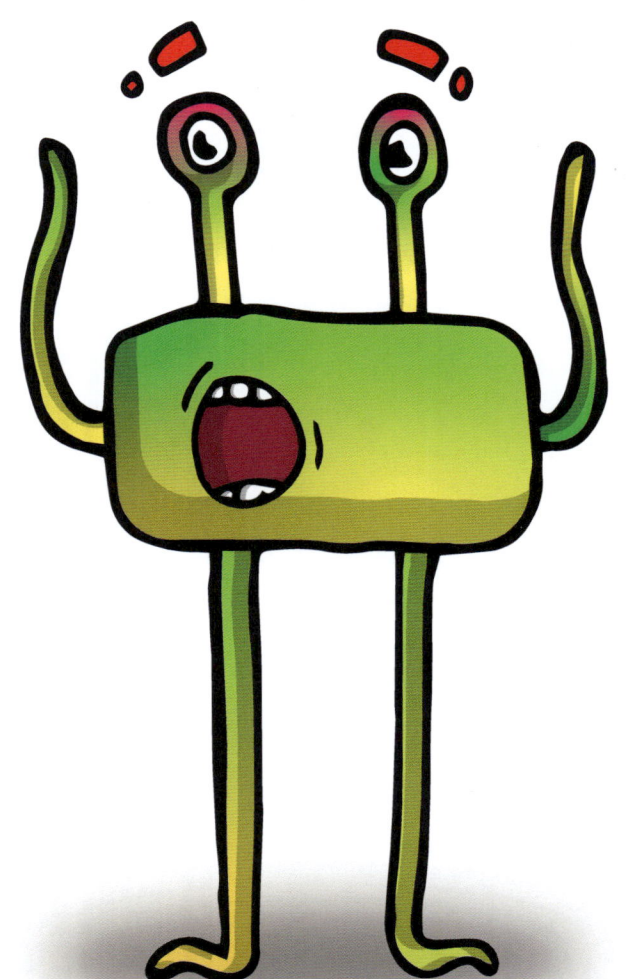

And that's okay.

When you are surprised you might want to...

Not speak	Jump in the air	Smile

You might feel like you can't talk.

You might feel like you want to jump in the air.

You might feel excited.

You might feel surprised if your friend came to visit and you didn't know.

I'm hurt...

And that's okay.

When you are hurt you might want to...

Shout

Not speak

Cry

Your chest might feel tight.

You might feel sick.

You might have a hurt head.

You might feel hurt if someone has said something mean.

When you are bored you might want to...

Fall asleep	Do something	Moan

You might feel like sleeping.

You might feel like you want to move.

You might feel grumpy.

You might feel bored if you have to watch something on TV you don't like.

I'm nervous...

And that's okay.

When you are nervous you might want to...

Not speak

Hide

Run away

You might feel scared.

You might feel sick.

You might breathe fast.

You might feel nervous if you are part of your school play.

When you are jealous you might want to...

Moan

Hide

Not speak

You might feel grumpy.

You might feel like not joining in.

You might feel sad.

You might feel jealous if your friend gets the toy you want.

I'm disappointed...

And that's okay.

When you are disappointed you might want to...

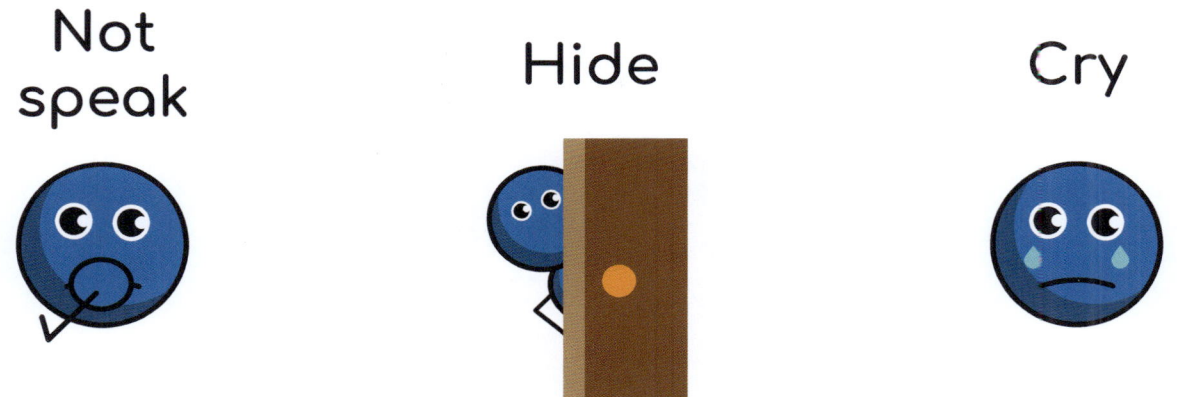

You might feel sleepy.

You might feel sad.

You might feel like not moving.

You might feel disappointed if a cake you make comes out too small.

I'm angry!

And that's okay.

When you are **angry** you might want to...

Shout

Run away

Cry

You might **have a hurt head.**

You might **feel hot.**

You might **scream.**

You might feel angry if someone broke your toy.

I'm embarrassed.

And that's okay.

When you are embarrassed you might want to...

Not speak

Hide

Run away

You might feel like not joining in.

You might feel hot.

You might feel nervous.

You might feel embarrassed if you get someone's name wrong.

That's Okay!

It's normal to not feel an emotion.

It's normal to feel an emotion.

Emotions come and go.

And that's okay!

thatsokay.co.uk

© 2022 Chris Dixon. All rights reserved.

Printed in Great Britain
by Amazon